HOW TO IMPROVE AT
JUDO

All the information you need to know to get on top of your game!

Ashley P Martin is a martial arts and sports writer. His titles include The Shotokan Karate Bible, The Advanced Shotokan Karate Bible and How to Improve at Karate. He is also the Chief Instructor and Grading Examiner of Just Karate (www.justkarate.co.uk) based in Cambridge, England.

More than just instructional guides, the **HOW TO IMPROVE AT...** series gives you everything you need to achieve your goals—tips on technique, step-by-step demonstrations, nutritional advice, and the secrets of successful pro athletes. Excellent visual instructions and expert advice combine to act as your own personal trainer. These books aim to give you the know-how and confidence to improve your performance.

Studies have shown that an active approach to life makes you feel happier and less stressed. The easiest way to start is by taking up a new sport or improving your skills in an existing one. You simply have to choose an activity that enthuses you.

HOW TO IMPROVE AT JUDO does not promise instant success. It simply gives you the tools to become the best at whatever you choose to do.

Every care has been taken to ensure that these instructions are safe to follow, but in the event of injury Crabtree Publishing shall not be liable for any injuries or damages.

ticktock Media Ltd. would like to thank Wolverhampton Youth Judo Centre for their help with this title.

Left to right:
Keith Jones (coach), Winston, Ashley, Dylan, Debbie Cox (coach), (front) Selina, Heather.

Crabtree Publishing Company
www.crabtreebooks.com

Author: Ashley Martin
Editors: John Crossingham, Annabel Savery
Proofreader: Adrianna Morganelli
Project coordinator: Robert Walker
Prepress technician: Margaret Amy Salter
Production coordinator: Margaret Amy Salter
Designer: Graham Rich
Managing Editor: Rachel Tisdale
Photographer: Chris Fairclough

Consultant:
Eric G Bartlett is a 4th degree black belt who has 56 years experience in studying and teaching judo.
Photo credits:
Getty Images: Koichi Kamoshida: p. 46; Jonathan Ferrey: p. 47 (top); Jacques Demarthon: p. 47 (middle); Clive Brunskill: p. 47 bottom

Planning and production by Discovery Books Ltd.

Library and Archives Canada Cataloguing-in-Publication

Martin, Ashley P., 1972-
    How to improve at judo / Ashley P. Martin.

(How to improve at--)
Includes index.
ISBN 978-0-7787-3574-8 (bound).--ISBN 978-0-7787-3596-0 (pbk.)

    1. Judo--Training--Juvenile literature. I. Title. II. Series: How to improve at--

GV1114.M76 2009   j796.815'2   C2008-907843-8

Library of Congress Cataloging-in-Publication Data

Martin, Ashley.
  How to improve at judo / Ashley P. Martin.
      p. cm. -- (How to improve at--)
  Includes index.
    ISBN 978-0-7787-3596-0 (pbk. : alk. paper) -- ISBN 978-0-7787-3574-8
(reinforced library binding : alk. paper)
  1. Judo--Juvenile literature. I. Title.
  GV1114.M77 2009
  796.815'2--dc22

                2008052119

Crabtree Publishing Company
www.crabtreebooks.com   1-800-387-7650

Published in Canada
Crabtree Publishing
616 Welland Ave.
St. Catharines, Ontario
L2M 5V6

Published in the United States
Crabtree Publishing
PMB16A
350 Fifth Ave., Suite 3308
New York, NY 10118

CONTENTS

INTRODUCTION

Judo is a martial art. Students of judo are known as judoka. In competitions, judoka score points for throwing an opponent to the ground, or subduing an opponent using a grappling technique. In Japanese, judo means "the gentle way". It gets this name because judoka use an opponent's attacks against that opponent.

WHERE JUDO COMES FROM

Judo comes from Japan where it was created by Jigoro Kano in 1882. Kano based judo on jujitsu, the traditional unarmed fighting style of Japanese warriors, or samurai. He removed the more dangerous techniques from jujitsu, such as punching and kicking.

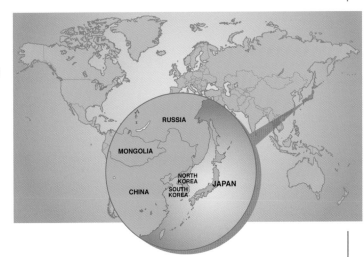

JUDO AS AN OLYMPIC SPORT

Judo has been an Olympic sport for men since the 1964 Toyko Games. In 1988, it was made a demonstration sport for women. It became an official Olympic women's event in 1992.

GUIDE TO ARROWS & SYMBOLS

Throughout the book we have used red arrows like this ⬌ to indicate the action and direction of the body.

We have also used circles to highlight key hand or foot actions.

This symbol ⊢⊣ indicates the correct distance between your feet.

EQUIPMENT FOR TRAINING

The Judo uniform is called a judogi, or gi. It is traditionally made from heavy white cotton. In competitions, one competitor will wear a white gi and the other will wear a blue gi to make it easier to tell them apart. The judogi has no buttons or zippers. It is tied together with only a belt. If it gets pulled open nothing will rip.

HYGIENE AND SAFETY

Hygiene and safety are important in Judo.
- *Keep the nails on your fingers and toes short*
- *Do not wear any jewelry*
- *Tie back long hair*
- *Make sure that both you and your judogi are clean – bad body odor is even against the rules in judo competitions!*

BELT

The gi is held together with a belt. The color of the belt signifies grade. Most belts are made of dyed cotton. Some black belts are white cotton coated with black silk. It is important to tie your belt correctly — this is one of the first things to learn when you start training.

JUDO MATS

Judo should be practiced on mats, or tatami. Traditional tatami were made of compressed rice straw wrapped in soft woven rush straw. Today, mats are made of foam covered by colored vinyl. Students are expected to help lay out mats before each lesson and to put them away at the end. Judo mats can be heavy so carry them with a friend.

Judo practices often involve falling on the floor so mats are used. Some judo mats have jigsaw edges so that they fit together tightly.

THE JUDO BELT

The growth of a judoka — from beginner to expert — is tracked using the colored belt system starting at white through to black. Each belt requires the performance of a specific syllabus at a grading examination. If you do enough training then you will usually be able to take a grading every three months. By training regularly, most people are able to get to black belt in three to five years. The belt system varies from one country to another but the most common order in which belts are awarded is:

JUDO BELT SYSTEM

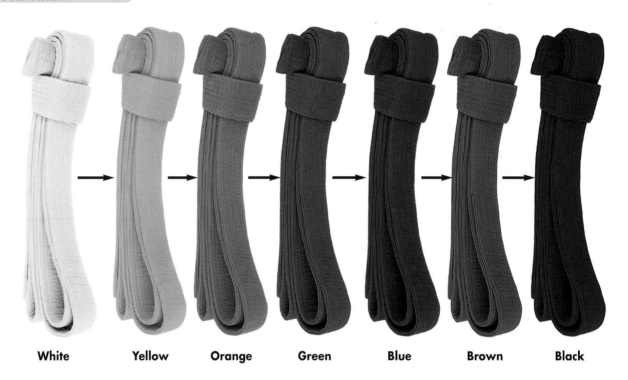

| White | Yellow | Orange | Green | Blue | Brown | Black |

ABOVE BLACK BELT

The black belt is a great accomplishment. There are ten degrees of black belt. The first degree is known as shodan, which means "first level." High ranking judo experts usually wear a black belt, but other colored belts can be worn. Red and white belts are often worn by 6th, 7th and 8th degree black belts. At 9th and 10th level a red belt can be worn.

1st - 5th degree black belt = **Black**

6th - 8th degree black belt = **Red and white**

9th - 10th degree black belt = **Red**

Center point

STEP 1
Fold the belt in half, so that you find the center.

STEP 2
Place the center on your stomach.

STEP 3
Wrap the belt around your waist so that the ends cross over behind your back.

STEP 4
Keep wrapping the belt so that both ends come around front. Hold the two ends together near your middle.

STEP 5
Pass the right-hand end under the belt that you are holding in the middle.

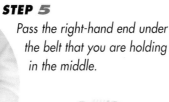

STEP 6
Now tie a simple knot in the belt and pull both ends tight.

THE JUDO DOJO

*T*he "dojo" is the name given to any place where judo training takes place. Training can happen almost anywhere. Sometimes judo is even done outside in good weather. Usually, judo is done in a sports hall or a custom built dojo with mats on the floor. When you enter the dojo proper behavior is expected.

Practicing judo is fun but it can be dangerous if you are not careful. Always treat your teacher and training partners with respect.

BOWING

STANDING BOW

STEP 1
Stand with your heels together and your toes pointing out diagonally.

STEP 2
Put your hands on your thighs and bend at the waist.

SITTING BOW

STEP 1
Start in a kneeling position.

STEP 2
Place your hands in front of your knees. Make a diamond shape with your thumbs and index fingers almost touching. Bow by bending at the waist.

WHEN TO BOW

Bowing is important because it shows respect and helps clear the mind before training. You should also bow:

• Upon entering or exiting the competition area.
• Before the class begins and after the class ends.
• Before and after working with a partner.

THE INSTRUCTOR

Judo classes are usually taught by a black belt instructor. The instructor is called "sensei," which is Japanese for "teacher."

• Pay attention to what your sensei tells you. Be especially aware of instructions regarding safety.
• If you are late for a session, wait for the instructor to allow you to join in.

THE COMPETITION AREA

While judo training can be done any place, official competitions are held on a matted contest area. This area is bordered by the danger area. The danger area is usually red. Competitors must stay inside the contest area. Stepping out of this area results in a warning. A competitor who repeatedly steps out of the contest area loses points.

THE OFFICIALS

Judges' chairs
A referee and two judges control a judo match. Judges use flags to indicate that a point is being scored or if a rule is being broken.

Score table
The contest sheet writer, the scoreboard keeper and the timekeeper are seated at the score table. They keep track of the score and tell the referee when time is up.

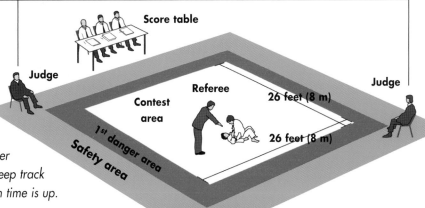

Judges' chairs

Score table

Judge

Judge

Referee

Contest area

26 feet (8 m)

26 feet (8 m)

1st danger area

Safety area

KEY INSTRUCTIONS DURING A JUDO CONTEST

The referee gives various instructions, often in Japanese. These are the most important ones:
HAJIME – *Start. You must wait for the referee to say "hajime" before you can start or resume fighting.*

MATTE – *Wait. When the referee announces "matte," both competitors stop fighting immediately.*

IPPON – *Full point. This wins the match.*

WAZA-ARI – *Half point.*

YUKO – *A score less than "waza-ari."*

KOKA – *A score less than "yuko."*

OSAEKOMI – *A contestant is being held in a pin by an opponent.*

PREPARE TO PLAY

Judo can be a tough sport. Make sure that you do five to ten minutes of warm-up exercises before training. This helps to prepare your body and can reduce the chance of injuries. Start your warm-up with slower movements at first and then gradually increase the intensity of your activity.

KNEE BEND

STEP 1
Place your feet shoulder width apart.

STEP 2
Drop your weight by bending your knees. Now straighten your legs.

KNEE LIFT

Stand with your feet shoulder width apart. Bring your knee as close to your shoulder as possible. Repeat this exercise several times then switch to your other leg.

UPPER BODY ROTATION

STEP 1
Stand with your feet shoulder width apart. Put your arms up in front of you with your elbows bent.

STEP 2
Rotate slowly side to side. Let your feet twist as you turn, lifting the heel of your rear foot.

FORWARD STRETCH

STEP 1
Stand with your feet shoulder width apart. Reach up above your head as high as you can.

STEP 2
Keeping your legs straight, bend at your waist and stretch to the ground.

STOMACH CRUNCH

STEP 1
Lie on your back with your knees bent and feet flat on the floor. Put your hands on your thighs.

STEP 2
Lift your upper body so that your hands reach up toward your knees. Don't lift your knees up.

NECK STRETCH

STEP 1
Stand with a straight back. Slowly drop your chin to your chest, then lift your chin and look up.

STEP 2
Slowly look to the left and then to the right.

STEP 3
Look forward and then slowly turn your head to the side so that your ear comes toward your shoulder. Repeat to the opposite side.

BREAKFALLS

An essential part of judo is learning how to fall correctly. This is called a breakfall, or ukemi. By practicing breakfalls, you can reduce the risk of injury when you are thrown. Ukemi skills also give you an advantage in a judo match. Your opponent won't score as highly if you perform a proper breakfall when you are thrown.

BACKWARD BREAKFALL FROM CROUCH POSITION

STEP 1
Start low with your knees bent. Drop your chin to your chest. Extend your arms in front of you with your hands open.

Keep your chin close to your chest.

STEP 2
Drop backward.

Slap the mat with both hands.

STEP 3
As your upper back touches the mat, bring your arms out to the side so that you slap the mat with your arms and hands.

TOP TIP
When you are doing a backward breakfall, make sure that you keep your arms straight.

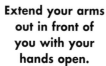

Extend your arms out in front of you with your hands open.

STEP 1
Start by dropping your chin to your chest.

STEP 2
Bend your knees and drop your hips.

Once you are confident with a backward breakfall from the crouch position, you can try falling from a standing position.

Keep your chin close to your chest.

STEP 3
Drop backward. As your upper back touches the mat, bring your arms out to the sides of your body so that you slap the mat with your arms and open hands.

Rest your right hand on your belt.

Keep your chin tucked in to your chest.

STEP 1
Start in a kneeling position, resting on your right knee with your left foot flat on the floor.

Left hand on left knee

STEP 2
Slide your left foot to the right. Move your left hand to the right while keeping your right hand on your belt knot.

STEP 3
Keep your chin tucked in as you fall to the side.

As you land, slap the ground with your left arm and open hand.

TOP TIP
Slap the ground at the same instant that the rest of your body hits the mat.

FRONT BREAKFALLS

Breakfalling from the front is used when you are thrown forward either by a hip throw or a shoulder throw. Practicing breakfalls is essential. It builds up your reflexes so you can land safely during training and competition.

FRONT ROLLING BREAKFALL

STEP 1
Start with your left leg forward.

STEP 2
Bend your legs and reach to the ground, keeping your arms slightly bent.

Your hands should be open and just to the side of your front foot. Point your hands slightly toward each other with the right hand pointing back and the left pointing forward.

STEP 3
Push your weight forward and over your front foot. Tuck your head in and push with both of your legs so that you roll over your left shoulder.

Keep your head tucked in.

STEP 4
You should roll over onto your right hip. As you land, slap down with your right hand.

FRONT BREAKFALL FROM KNEELING

STEP 1
Kneel with both knees on the ground.

Hold your hands out in front of you, with the palms facing out and your wrists straight.

Keep your chin up and away from the mat during the fall.

STEP 2
Fall forward. Keep your elbows straight, landing on your palms and forearms on the mat.

FRONT BREAKFALL FROM STANDING

STEP 1
Bend your knees. Hold your hands up in front of you with the palms facing out and your wrists straight.

Bend knees

STEP 2
Fall forward and shoot your legs back, so you are on the balls of your feet. Keep your elbows straight and land on the mat using your palms and forearms.

Keep chin up and away from mat.

STEP 3
Keep your chin up, your legs straight and your hips raised. Only the balls of your feet, your forearms and hands touch the mat.

Only make contact with the mat with the balls of your feet, your forearms, and hands.

TAPPING OUT – HOW TO SUBMIT IN A JUDO CONTEST

Asubmission is a way of indicating to an opponent that you concede that they have successfully applied a technique and that you want them to stop. Being able to submit is important in judo practice sessions as well as in competitions because strangleholds and joint locks can be dangerous if applied too strongly and for too long. A submission allows you to acknowledge one of these techniques without allowing the technique to be damaging.

HOW TO SUBMIT

One way to submit is to say "Maitta," or "I submit." *However, if you are in a stranglehold, it will be difficult to say anything so it is more common in judo to submit by slapping the mat (known as* **tapping out***). It is essential that, if you have someone in a lock or hold, you immediately release them when they submit.*

You can submit by slapping the mat two or more times. If your hands aren't free to slap the mat then you can use your feet instead.

GRIPPING

*G*ood gripping technique (kumikata) is essential in judo. Your grip is your connection with your opponent. You will need to use your grip to try to control your opponent's movement and balance, and to get immediate feedback on your opponent's actions.

Both athletes stand with right legs forward.

Opponent

SYMMETRICAL GRIP *AIYOTSU*

STEP 1
Stand facing your opponent with your right leg forward. Your opponent also stands with their right leg forward.

STEP 2
Grip the right sleeve of your opponent's jacket with your left hand. Your opponent grabs your lapel with their right hand.

NON-SYMMETRICAL GRIP *KENKA YOTSU*

STEP 3
Grip the lapel of your opponent's jacket with your right hand.

Grip your opponent's jacket.

In the non-symmetrical grip, one fighter grips the sleeve with their right hand and one grips with their left.

Grip your opponent's sleeve.

HIP THROWS

Hip throws (koshi waza) make use of the hip as a pivot point, helping you to throw opponents who are heavier than you. Most hip throws take advantage of your opponent's forward motion to use their momentum against them.

FLOATING HIP THROW *UKI GOSHI*

This technique is one of the oldest judo throws and is also one of the easiest to learn.

STEP 1

Grab your opponent's sleeve with your left hand. Do not grab their lapel with your right hand, as you will need that arm free to reach around your opponent to do the throw.

STEP 2

Slide your right arm under your opponent's left arm and around to their lower back. At the same time, push your right hip into your opponent's body.

Make sure that there is good contact between your hip and your opponent.

Opponent

STEP 3

Twist your upper body so that your opponent rotates around your hip and is thrown to the ground.

STEP 4

Your opponent should break their fall with their free arm and hand by slapping the mat.

Opponent should breakfall out of throw.

TOP TIP
Do not bend your knees when doing this throw. Instead, use the twisting action to generate the power to throw your opponent.

LARGE HIP THROW O GOSHI

This basic technique is similar to the floating hip throw but uses a bigger and more powerful action that will throw your opponent over your hip rather than around it.

STEP 1

Grab your opponent's sleeve with your left hand. Do not grab their lapel with your right hand as you will need that arm free to reach around your opponent to do the throw.

Opponent

STEP 2

As your opponent pushes on you with their right hand, allow your body to rotate, pushing forward with your right shoulder and slipping your right hand under their left arm and behind their back.

Bend forward

STEP 3

Continue rotating so that you face away from your opponent, pushing your hips back toward them. Bend forward slightly, bringing their weight onto your hip.

STEP 4

Rotate your upper body and straighten your legs so that you throw your opponent over your hip.

Straighten legs

TOP TIP

As you bring your opponent's weight onto your hip, make sure that your knees are bent and that your feet and your head point forward.

LIFTING-PULLING HIP THROW *TSURIKOMI GOSHI*

This technique weakens your opponent's position by using a lifting action to try to move them onto their toes. This can be an effective way of throwing an opponent who stiffens up and pulls back in an effort to resist *uki goshi* or *o goshi*.

STEP 1
Start by gripping your opponent's sleeve with your left hand and their lapel with your right.

STEP 2
Step in so that your right hip moves close to your opponent. At the same time, while gripping tightly on the lapel, lift your opponent's jacket.

Bend your knees

STEP 3
Rotate so that you face away from your opponent.

Opponent

STEP 4
Rotate your upper body and pull your opponent over your hip, while straightening your knees.

TOP TIP
Make sure that you bend your knees so that you get as low as you can before finishing this throw.

This powerful technique is popular in judo tournaments. Although *harai goshi* is classified as a hip technique, it makes use of a sweeping action with the foot.

STEP 1

Grab your opponent's sleeve with your left hand. Do not grab their lapel with your right hand as you will need that arm free to reach around your opponent to do the throw.

Grab right shoulder

Opponent

STEP 2

Slide your right arm over your opponent's left shoulder and around their neck so that you can grab their right shoulder on the other side. At the same time, push your right hip into your opponent's body. Make sure that there is good contact between your hip and your opponent.

Push right hip into opponent.

Lift opponent up

Lift right foot and swing leg back.

STEP 3

Unbalance your opponent by lifting their weight up. Prepare to sweep by lifting your right foot.

STEP 4

Swing back with your right leg, sweeping your opponent's legs away. At the same time, drop your head and arms, throwing them over your hip.

TOP TIP

Make sure that you get really close to your opponent – you should feel like you are getting right underneath them when sweeping out their legs.

HIP WHEEL THROW *KOSHI GURUMA*

This technique involves pushing your hips right into your opponent so that you can roll them over you like a wheel.

Opponent

STEP 1

Grab your opponent's sleeve with your left hand. Do not grab the lapel with your right hand as you will need that arm free to reach around your opponent to do the throw.

STEP 2

As your opponent pushes on you with their right hand, allow your body to rotate, pushing forward with your right shoulder and slipping your right hand over their shoulder and behind their neck.

Push hips back towards opponent.

STEP 3

Continue rotating so that you face away from your opponent, pushing your hips back towards theirs. Bend forward slightly, bringing their weight onto your hip.

STEP 4

Rotate your upper body so that you throw your opponent over your hip and onto the mat.

TOP TIP
Make the hip rotation as big as possible so that it feels like you are going right past your opponent.

HIP SHIFT *UTSURI GOSHI*

Opponent

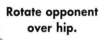

Unlike other hip throws, *utsuri goshi* can be used when you are behind your opponent and is therefore an effective counter attack against a hip or shoulder throw.

STEP 1

Start with your opponent in front of you with their left arm over your shoulder as if they are attempting to throw you.

Hold their right sleeve with your left hand.

Bend your knees so that you are ready to lift.

STEP 2

Lift your opponent to your right side while stepping forward slightly with your right foot so that your opponent swings round onto your right hip.

Lift opponent to right side.

Rotate opponent over hip.

STEP 4

Rotate to your right bringing your opponent off your hip with your right arm.

STEP 3

Rotate your upper body to your left, swinging your opponent over your hip so that their legs are behind you.

Your opponent should land on their back in front of you.

HAND THROWS

Hand throws (te waza) emphasize the use of your hands, arms and shoulders to throw your opponent. However, it is important to utilize the whole of your body when throwing. Some hand throws require that you use your legs or hips to assist the arm movement.

TWO-HANDED SHOULDER THROW *MOROTE SEOI NAGE*

This is one of the most popular throws and is very common in judo tournaments.

STEP 1
Start by gripping your opponent's sleeve with your left hand and their lapel with your right.

Opponent

STEP 2
Step in towards your opponent with your right foot so that you are sideways on with your knees bent. While maintaining your grip on your opponent's jacket, push your right elbow toward your opponent's right armpit.

Step in

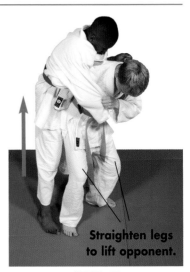

Straighten legs to lift opponent.

STEP 3
Rotate so that you are facing away from your opponent and lift them by straightening your legs, taking their weight on your back and right forearm.

STEP 4
Keep rotating to your right so that you throw your opponent over your shoulder.

TOP TIP
Make sure you bend your knees so that you can get as low as you can before finishing this throw.

ONE-ARM SHOULDER THROW *IPPON SEOI NAGE*

This is a variation of the two-handed shoulder throw. As you do not need to grip your opponent's *judogi* they do not need to be wearing one. Therefore, it is an important self-defense move.

STEP 1

Grab your opponent's sleeve with your left hand. Do not grab their lapel with your right hand as you will need that arm free to reach around your opponent to do the throw.

Opponent

STEP 2

As your opponent pushes on you with their right hand, allow your body to rotate. Slide in and turn right around so that you push your hips right into your opponent. At the same time, bring your right hand under their right arm.

Bend your knees

Straighten legs to lift opponent.

STEP 3

Lift your opponent by bringing their weight onto your right shoulder and straighten your legs.

STEP 4

Twist your body and throw your opponent around your right shoulder.

TOP TIP

Before throwing your opponent, try to lift them onto your shoulders.

BODY DROP *TAI OTOSHI*

This popular technique is best used when your opponent is moving forward and can be used as an attacking move or a counter-attacking move. Although *tai otoshi* is classified as a hand technique, it makes use of a blocking action that uses the leg to help unbalance your opponent.

STEP 1

Start by gripping your opponent's sleeve with your left hand and their lapel with your right.

STEP 2

As your opponent makes a forward motion, step back with your left leg pulling them off balance.

STEP 3

Rotate and step back with your left foot.

STEP 4

Pull your opponent forward and put your right leg out in front of them.

Opponent

Pull opponent over right leg.

STEP 5

Rotate and pull your opponent over your leg, throwing them to the ground.

TOP TIP
Ensure that you have a stable base by keeping your legs far apart.

HAND WHEEL *TE GURUMA*

This technique is often classified as a "pick-up" because it involves picking up your opponent and then dropping them. *Te guruma* is particularly effective as a counter attack against a large outer reap (see page 30) or a sweeping hip throw.

Opponent

STEP 1
Start with your right hand gripping your opponent's lapel but do not let them get a high grip on your jacket.

Duck under arm

STEP 2
As your opponent tries to get a high grip, duck under their arm and step in close so that your right shoulder is tucked under their right armpit and their right foot is between your feet. Keep your knees bent and reach low around behind your opponent with your left arm.

Step in close

Bend knees

Opponent's right foot is between your feet.

Lift opponent

STEP 4
As you lift with your left arm, let your right arm drop as if you are turning a big wheel. This will roll your opponent in the air so that they land onto their back.

STEP 3
With your left hand grab the inside of your opponent's right leg and lift them off the ground. Your right hand should still be on your opponent's lapel.

TOP TIP
When you go in to grab your opponent, try to dash in as quickly as you can to maintain the element of surprise.

LEG THROWS

Leg throws (ashi waza) use the legs or feet to unbalance an opponent so that they can be thrown. Rather than lifting your opponent, the idea is to *sweep* your opponent's feet away from under them.

ADVANCING FOOT SWEEP *DEASHI HARAI*

Opponent

This technique is easy to learn but difficult to make work in practice. You should use this technique when your opponent is moving forwards.

STEP 1

Start by gripping your opponent's sleeve with your left hand and their lapel with your right.

Intercept opponent's foot

STEP 2

As your opponent steps forward with their right foot, intercept it with your left foot.

STEP 3

Sweep out your opponent's right foot with your left foot. At the same time, pull with your left arm and push with your right, to unbalance them to their right side.

TOP TIP
The key to this foot sweep is timing. You have to wait until your opponent has committed to the forward motion but hasn't yet put their weight down fully on their foot.

Opponent

SMALL CIRCLE SWEEP *KOUCHI GARI*

The small circle sweep, also known as the small inner reap, can be used when your opponent is stepping forward or when they have their feet spread far apart.

Step forward

STEP 3
Move in toward your opponent so that you are sideways on, with your right hip close to your opponent. Lift your right foot ready to sweep to the left.

Lift right foot to sweep.

STEP 1
Start by gripping your opponent's sleeve with your left hand and their lapel with your right.

STEP 2
Push your opponent off balance to the rear by pushing with your right hand while pulling to your left with your left hand.

STEP 4
Sweep your opponent's right foot with your right foot.

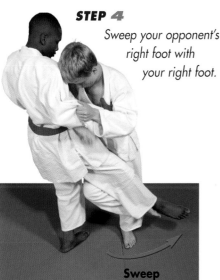

Sweep

STEP 5
You will unbalance your opponent and they will fall to the ground.

TOP TIP
Make sure that you get in close and sweep forward, in the opposite direction that you are pushing your opponent. Don't try to sweep your opponent's foot to the side.

LARGE OUTER REAP *OSOTO GARI*

This powerful throw "reaps" your opponent's foot from under them.

Opponent

STEP 1

Start by gripping your opponent's sleeve with your left hand and their lapel with your right.

STEP 2

Step past your opponent with your right leg while using your arms to unbalance them toward their right and to the rear. Then lift your right leg, ready to sweep backward.

Unbalance opponent

Make sure your feet and head are pointing out in the same direction.

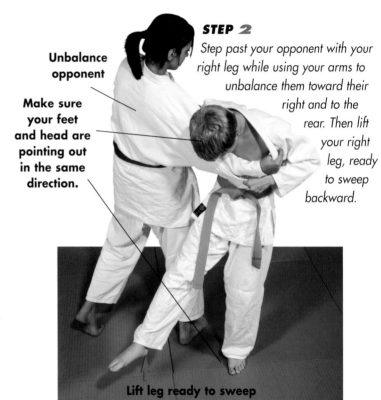

Lift leg ready to sweep

STEP 3

Bring your right leg back strongly to sweep out your opponent's right leg. At the same time, using your arms, bring your opponent around you, and then down.

Sweep leg back

STEP 4

Your opponent will land on their back in front of you.

TOP TIP

Make sure that your opponent is off balance before you try the actual sweeping action. If you fail to break your opponent's balance then there is a chance that they will be able to perform a counter throw on you.

Opponent

This technique, like *osoto gari*, reaps out your opponent's foot. It is often used in combination with *kouchi gari* because it starts with your foot in the same central position.

STEP 1

Start by gripping your opponent's sleeve with your left hand and their lapel with your right.

STEP 2

Pull down with your right hand so that you break your opponent's balance to their left side.

Break opponent's balance

Move in toward your opponent so that you are sideways on, with your right hip close to your opponent.

STEP 3

Hook your right leg in behind your opponent's left leg.

STEP 4

Pull your right leg back so that you sweep your opponent's left foot away, bringing them to the floor.

Hook right leg behind opponent's leg.

TOP TIP

Make sure that you use a committed movement to complete this technique. This will probably mean that you will fall with your opponent but this is fine because you will land on top and have the advantage.

SACRIFICE THROWS

Sacrifice throws (sutemi waza) are throws that involve dropping your weight to the floor, thereby sacrificing your standing posture in order to bring down your opponent. These throws are useful because they allow you to make use of your body weight rather than relying on your strength. However, a failed sacrifice throw can put you in a weak position.

CIRCULAR THROW *TOMOE NAGE*

— Opponent

You should use this technique when your opponent is moving towards you and, instead of resisting, you give way. *Tomoe nage* has been very popular with stunt coordinators for film and television, possibly because it looks impressive with your opponent being thrown right over you.

STEP 2

As your opponent advances, drop your weight back and lift your left foot into your opponent's stomach.

STEP 3

Drop onto your back and lift your opponent's hips into the air with your leg while pulling their upper body down and slightly to your right with your grip.

STEP 1

Start by gripping your opponent's sleeve with your right hand and their lapel with your left.

STEP 4

Your opponent tumbles over you, landing behind and slightly to the right of you.

TOP TIP
The higher your grip on your opponent's jacket, the more leverage you will get when throwing them.

Opponent

This technique can be used as an effective counter attack to a hip or shoulder throw. It makes use of a block with one leg while using all of your weight to bring down your opponent.

STEP 2

Release your left hand grip and bring your hand over your opponent's right arm and around behind their back. At the same time, move your weight forward so that your chest pushes into their right shoulder.

Get a good grip by grabbing the jacket or belt.

STEP 1

Start by gripping your opponent's sleeve with your left hand and their lapel with your right.

Move weight forward.

STEP 3

Drive your left leg behind your opponent, right past both of their legs. Immediately drop your weight to your left so that your opponent is unbalanced, falling over your left leg.

Drive your left leg behind both your opponent's legs.

STEP 4

As you land, twist so that you bring your weight on top of your opponent.

PINNING

*I*n judo, a *pinning* **technique** (osaekomi waza) *is one that holds an opponent on the ground and prevents them from getting up. In a judo competition, for a pin to score, you have to be on top of your opponent, either facing down or on your side. In addition, your opponent must be on their back and you cannot be between their legs.*

SCARF HOLD *KESA GATAME*

Use this technique to hold your opponent down by wrapping your arm around your opponent's head and body like a scarf.

Trap opponent's arm

Opponent

STEP 1
Start with your opponent on their back. Sit with your right hip against their right side and with their right arm over your legs.

Grab the shoulder part of their jacket and position your knee under their shoulder.

STEP 2
Seize your opponent's arm so that they can't move it. Do this by grabbing the shoulder part of their jacket with your left hand and positioning your right knee under their shoulder.

STEP 3
Wrap your right arm all the way underneath your opponent's neck.

TOP TIP
For extra control of your opponent's neck and head, grab your own right knee with your right hand.

SHOULDER HOLD *KATA GATAME*

This technique is one of the most effective holds in judo, and once applied it can be used as a choke.

STEP 1

Wrap your arm around your opponent's neck, trapping their right arm by tightly holding your neck against their upper arm.

STEP 1

Start with your opponent on their back. Sit on their left-hand side facing towards their stomach.

Opponent

SIDE FOUR-CORNER HOLD *YOKO SHIHO GATAME*

This pin primarily uses your body weight to hold your opponent down by holding your chest down on your opponent's chest or stomach.

STEP 2

Drop your chest down onto your opponent's stomach.

STEP 3

Wrap your left arm around the top of your opponent's thigh and lock it in place by grabbing your opponent's belt or the bottom of their jacket. Put your right arm under your opponent's neck and grab their jacket.

TOP TIP

To escape from this hold, hook your right leg over your opponent's head. From here you can get your opponent into a stranglehold using your legs.

STRAIGHT FOUR-CORNER HOLD *TATE SHIHO GATAME*

This pin primarily uses your body weight to hold your opponent down by sitting on their abdomen. In addition you should use your legs to control your opponent.

STEP 1

Start with your opponent on their back. Sit on their right-hand side facing toward their stomach.

STEP 2

Bring your right leg over your opponent's waist so that you're sitting above them with one leg either side of their body.

STEP 3

Bring your chest down to your opponent's chest and bring your right arm under their left armpit and your left arm under their neck.

Grab your right wrist with your left hand to lock arms in position.

Your hands should meet under your opponent's left shoulder.

VARIATION *KASURE SHIHO GATAME*

There are many variations of this hold. One variation involves trapping both of your opponent's arms. Your opponent's arms are trapped between your shoulder and their own head.

Apply pressure by locking your hands behind their neck.

TOP TIP

Don't let your opponent escape by rolling you off to one side. Keep your knees as wide as possible and be ready to use your arms to counter any escape attempts.

Practice this technique for escaping from pins. It uses the leg and back muscles to allow you to roll your opponent over.

STEP 1

Start by lying on your back with your feet flat on the ground and your hands palm up alongside your head.

STEP 2

Bridge onto your shoulders by lifting your hips off the ground.

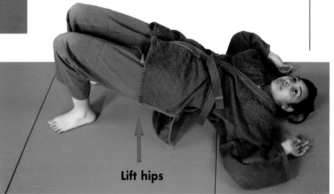

Lift hips

Bring right knee over

STEP 3

While maintaining the bridge by keeping your hips up as much as you can, drop your left shoulder and knee bringing your right knee over to the left.

Drop left shoulder

STEP 4

Rotate your hips so that your right leg travels over your left and you end up on your front.

CHOKE HOLDS

Choke holds (shime waza) apply pressure to the neck. Extreme caution must be used when learning choke holds because their application can be dangerous. Children are usually not permitted to use choking or strangling techniques in judo tournaments and should only learn these techniques under the supervision of an experienced instructor.

NORMAL CROSS LOCK *NAMI JIME*

STEP 1

Start with your opponent on their back. Sit on their stomach, facing them with your knees on either side of their body.

Opponent

STEP 2

Grab your opponent's left collar high up by the side of their neck with your left hand so that your hand is palm side down (your thumb will be inside the jacket and your four fingers will be on the outside).

STEP 3

Cross your right hand over your left and grip your opponent's right collar, again palm-side down so that your thumb is on the inside.

Apply the choke by spreading your elbows and pulling on the collar.

TOP TIP
This technique works best if you bring your head and chest close to your opponent.

STEP 1

Start with both you and your opponent on the ground. You should be sitting behind your opponent, holding on with your legs.

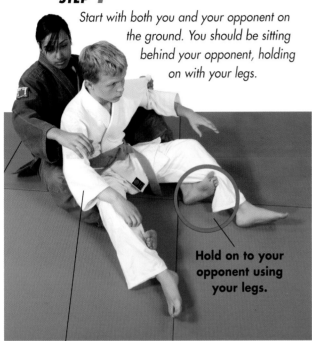

Opponent

Hold on to your opponent using your legs.

This technique is good to use if your opponent turns their back on you, for example when they are attempting a throw.

STEP 2

Reach around under your opponent's left arm with your left hand and grab the left lapel. Pull it tight.

STEP 3

Reach around your opponent's neck with your right arm and grab the left collar high up near to the neck.

STEP 4

Release your grip with your left hand and now grab the right lapel. Pull down with your left hand and up with your right to apply the strangle.

WARNING!

Choke holds should only be used under the supervision of an experienced instructor.

JOINT LOCKS

*J*oint locks (kansetsu waza) *involve the application of pressure to joints in such a way that they are pushed beyond their normal range. Because of the potentially damaging nature of joint locks, only elbow locks are allowed in competition. You should apply the joint lock with precision and, when your opponent indicates that they submit, it is important to release the lock immediately. If you find yourself in a joint lock, then you should not hesitate to tap out as soon as you feel the lock begin to engage.*

ENTANGLED ARM LOCK *UDE GARAMI*

STEP 1

Start with your opponent on their back. Sit on their right-hand side facing toward their chest.

Opponent

STEP 2

Drop your chest down onto your opponent's chest and grab your opponent's left wrist with your left hand.

STEP 3

Pass your right hand under your opponent's left arm and grab your left wrist to lock it in position.

Pull your opponent's hand toward you to apply the lock.

TOP TIP

This technique is applied on the elbow and not the shoulder, so it is important to remember to keep your opponent's arm bent.

CROSS ARM LOCK *UDE HISHIGI JUJI GATAME*

STEP 1

Start with your opponent on your left side on the ground. You should be standing with your left foot against their back, holding their left arm vertically, as if following a successful throw.

Hold opponent's left arm up with your right arm.

Opponent

STEP 2

Keep hold of your opponent's arm and step across their head so that your right foot is alongside their right shoulder.

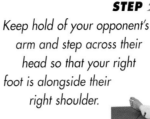

Step over head with right foot.

Sit down

STEP 3

Sit down and keep a tight hold on your opponent's arm using both of your arms.

Lean back

STEP 4

To get your opponent to tap out, keep their arm tight and lean back.

Lift hips

STEP 5

If necessary, you can apply more pressure to your opponent's elbow by bridging – keep contact with the ground with your shoulders but lift your hips off the ground.

WINNING A POINT

You can win a point in judo in any of the following ways:

Throwing your opponent
You can score a point for throwing your opponent
under the following circumstances:

• Your opponent must land mostly on their back.

• Your opponent must land with considerable force and speed.

Pinning your opponent
You can score a point by holding your opponent on the ground.
You can change the hold as many times as you want, as long
as these requirements are met:

• Your opponent is held largely on their back for 25 seconds.

• Your opponent must not have their legs wrapped around your legs or body.

Applying an arm lock or choke hold
You can score a point by applying an arm lock or choke hold if ANY of
the following happen:

• Your opponent gives up by tapping twice or more with their hand or foot.

• Your opponent gives up by saying "Maitta" ("I submit").

• Your opponent becomes unconscious.
  (For safety reasons chokes are not permitted on junior competitors).

**You can win a point
in judo by sucessfully
throwing an opponent.**

TIMING

**The time alloted for a judo contest varies from one competition to the next,
but for World Championships and the Olympic Games, the following times are allowed:**

Senior men and women (age 16+)   **5 minutes**
Junior men and women (under 16)   **4 minutes**
Only actual fighting time is counted—the timer is stopped during any interruptions to play.

WEIGHT CATEGORIES

These are the weight categories that have been in force since 1998:

(Table: Maximum weights allowed by category)	Men	Women
Extra Lightweight	60 kg (132 lbs)	48 kg (106 lbs)
Half Lightweight	66 kg (146 lbs)	52 kg (115 lbs)
Lightweight	73 kg (161 lbs)	57 kg (126 lbs)
Half-Middleweight	81 kg (179 lbs)	63 kg (139 lbs)
Middleweight	90 kg (198 lbs)	70 kg (154 lbs)
Half-Heavyweight	100 kg (220 lbs)	78 kg (172 lbs)
Heavyweight	over 100 kg (220 lbs)	over 78 kg (172 lbs)

Judo competitions have four types of points. From the highest to the lowest these are: *ippon*, *waza-ari*, *yuko*, *koka*. If you score an *ippon* or two *waza-aris*, you win immediately. If the time signal is given for the end of the contest and there is no *ippon* or equivalent scored, then the winner will be decided based on the other score categories:

(1) The number of waza-aris are considered – one waza-ari prevails over any number of yukos.

(2) If this still does not determine a winner then yukos will be counted – one yuko prevails over any number of kokas.

(3) If yukos are equal then kokas are counted.

IPPON

If you score a point, satisfying all the requirements, then you will score an ippon, and you will immediately be declared the winner.

WAZA-ARI

If you score a point, but partially fail to meet one of the requirements for an ippon, you will score a waza-ari. If you subsequently score another waza-ari then the referee will announce "waza-ari-awasete-ippon" which basically means that the two waza-ari add up to give you an ippon and you win. You will score a waza-ari under the following conditions:

Throw
If you throw your opponent with force and speed but they only partially land on their back then you will score a waza-ari.

Pin
You pin your opponent, meeting the same requirements as for an ippon but the hold lasts for more than 20 seconds but less than 25 seconds.

Arm lock or choke hold
You cannot score a waza-ari for an arm lock or a choke hold. Either your opponent submits, and you score an ippon, or they do not submit, and you score nothing.

YUKO

If you score a point but partially fail to meet the requirements for a waza-ari, you may score a yuko under the following conditions:

Throw
If you throw your opponent partially, lacking in speed or force, and they only land partially on their back then you will score a yuko.

Pin
You pin your opponent, meeting the same requirements as for an ippon but the hold lasts for more than 15 seconds but less than 20 seconds.

KOKA

If you score a point but partially fail to meet the requirements for a yuko, you may score a koka under the following conditions:

Throw
If you throw your opponent with speed and force but they land on their thigh, buttocks or one shoulder then you will score a koka.

Pin
You pin your opponent, meeting the same requirements as for an ippon but the hold lasts for more than 10 seconds but less than 15 seconds.

CONTEST TIME

2:00

Home | Visitor

I W Y K   I W Y K

1 0 0 1   1 2 3

You can score a *waza-ari*, *yuko* or a *koka* by pinning your opponent.

DIET & MENTAL ATTITUDE

A healthy diet during judo training and competitions can give you the edge. Energy from eating the correct diet means that you can improve your performance.

This diagram shows the percentage of foods that should be eaten to maintain a balanced diet.

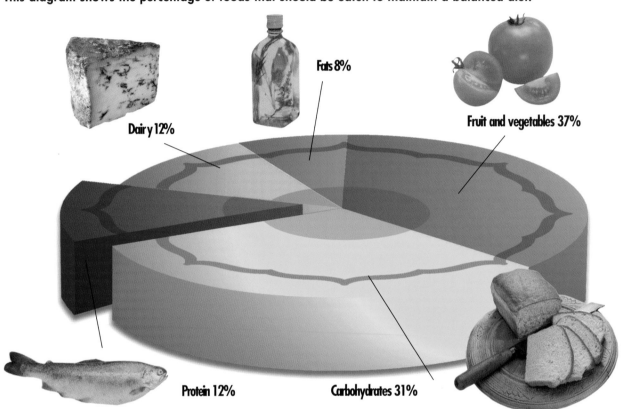

Dairy 12%

Fats 8%

Fruit and vegetables 37%

Protein 12%

Carbohydrates 31%

BEFORE EXERCISE

Eat high carbohydrate meals. Judo training sessions normally last between one and two hours.

Snacks eaten within an hour before exercise should keep you from feeling hungry. Judo competitions on the other hand tend to be all day events with many breaks. So it's best to keep carbohydrate snacks like bananas and sandwiches close at hand.

DURING EXERCISE

Judo can be hot work and so it's important to stay hydrated.

It is a good idea to hydrate before beginning any exercise and then to re-hydrate regularly after the first 30 minutes of exercise. Water is suitable for short training sessions, and sports drinks that contain sugars are more effective for longer training sessions.

While fitness, strength and technical skill are all essential components of judo, physical training is only a part of it. An essential component is your mental attitude. Training to become a black belt and training for competitions require patience and perseverance.

AWARENESS

You should be aware of your surroundings and your opponent.
The Japanese call this "Zanshin." You need to be aware of an imminent attack in order to react to it and to defend yourself.

OPEN MIND

Being aware of an imminent attack is not enough.
You must also be in the correct state of mind in order to react to that attack. This means that you need to have an open mind which is able to react to any attack. The Japanese call this "Mushin." If you build a plan around one particular attack then you will be unable to act quickly if that expectation is wrong.

CONCENTRATION

It is essential to maintain focus and keep your mind attentive to your opponent's movements.
One lapse in concentration is all it takes for your opponent to throw you, and one ippon is all it takes to finish a match.

PERSEVERANCE

Training to become a black belt can take anywhere between three and five years.
A typical student will train two to three times a week for this duration of time. Therefore, to become a proficient martial artist takes many years of training and commitment. Staying motivated and on track to achieve this goal is essential. Judo training is mostly about repeating moves until they start to become natural reactions.

COURTESY AND RESPECT

You should be polite to everyone, and that includes your opponents.
If you do not have respect for your opponent's abilities then you are in danger of under-estimating them. At the start of a judo contest, competitors are expected to bow to each other as a sign of this mutual respect.

HOW THE EXPERTS PLAY

There are many different types of judo competitions. The smallest are internal club competitions which only take one or two hours. The largest are international tournaments like the World Championships or the Olympic Games which take many days. In between, there are various regional and national tournaments which usually take one day.

TYPICAL TOURNAMENT DAY

7.00 a.m.	Wake up
7.30 a.m.	Eat high–energy breakfast
8.00 a.m.	Get on bus and travel to venue
9.15 a.m.	Arrive at venue and register
9.30 a.m.	Get changed
9.45 a.m.	Team warm-up and pep talk
10.00 a.m.	Tournament starts. Competitors wait for their events in preliminary rounds
4.00 p.m.	Final rounds
5.00 p.m.	Medals award ceremony
6.00 p.m.	Tournament finishes. Get back on bus and head home
7.30 p.m.	Team dinner. Reflect together on successes and areas for improvement

There are many different types of tournaments, from small local competitions all the way up to the big international events like the World Championships and the Olympics. Even if you are quite new to judo, there will be an opportunity for you to compete and many of the local and national events include a variety of age, grade, and skill levels.

Qualifying for the Olympics takes years of training, and most competitors would have started learning judo at a young age.

Valerie Gotay is one of the United States' top female competitors. She began competing at international level by the age of 14 and qualified for the U.S. Olympic Team in 1992 at the age of 18. She is a 4th degree black belt and won gold in the Pan-American Championships in 2008 in the lightweight (under 57 kg) category.

Craig Fallon (wearing blue) is the number one British judo competitor in the extra lightweight (under 60 kg) category.
In 2005, he won gold at the World Championships in Cairo.

At just 21 years of age Ishii Satoshi attended his first Olympic Games in Beijing in 2008 and won gold in the heavyweight (+100 kg) category.
He had previously won silver in the 2006 Doha Asian Games and won the All-Japan Judo Championships in 2006 and 2008.

GLOSSARY

BLOCK *A way of making your opponent fall by obstructing the movement of his or her leg so that they lose balance*

BREAKFALL *A way of landing following a fall so that you don't get hurt*

DOJO *The place where judo training takes place.*

GRAPPLING TECHNIQUE *A fighting technique that grabs or holds an opponent*

MOMENTUM *Any body that is moving has momentum in the direction that it is moving, and will tend to keep moving in that direction*

PIN *A move used to immobilize an opponent on the mat*

REAP *A leg technique that reaps or cuts away an opponent's leg from under them. This movement tends to be more vigorous than a sweep*

SACRIFICE THROW *A throw that involves giving up your standing posture in order to throw an opponent*

SWEEP *A leg technique intended to knock an opponent's foot or lower leg in order to unbalance ... A sweep usually refers to a technique that takes away an opponent's foot just as the weight is being transferred to it.*

TAPPING OUT *Indicating that you give up by tapping the ground*

THROW *A grappling move whereby an opponent is unbalanced or lifted so that can be tossed to the ground*

INDEX

JUN 19 2009

Printed in the U.S.A. — CG